THE ANGRY 30's

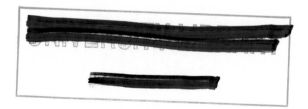

THE ANGRY 30's

JULIAN SYMONS

EYRE METHUEN LONDON

PICTURE CREDITS

Acknowledgements and thanks for permission to reproduce pictures are due to The Radio Times Hulton Picture Library for plates 2, 9, 14, 15, 19 to 22, 24, 32, 47, 53, 55, 56, 61, 65, 67, 69 to 71, 75, 87, 94, 96 to 98, 100, 101, 103, 104, 110, 112, 114, 115, 117, 118, 123, 124 and 127; to the *Daily Herald* for plates 25, 43, 45, 48, 58, 62, 64, 84, 86 and 125; to The Keystone Press Agency for plates 3, 5, 13, 72, 74, 77, 78, 92 and 121; to the Syndication International for plates 6, 7, 16, 41, 76 and 91; to The Klugmann Collection for plates 39, 81, 89, 90 and 122; to the Kodak Museum for plates 30, 34, 37, 51 and 66; to the Illustrated London News & Sketch Ltd for plates 4, 44, 85 and 116; to Birmingham City Libraries for plates 28, 33, 52 and 54; to Manchester Public Libraries for plates 26, 40, 120 and 126; to British Gas for plates 27, 31 and 99; to Leeds City Libraries for plates 102, 108 and 109; to the University of Reading Museum of English Rural Life for plates 18, 50 and 88; to Popperfoto for plates 10, 11 and 42; to British Railways for plates 105 and 106; to Central Press Photos Ltd for plates 38 and 93; to Merseyside County Museums for plates 29 and 35; to Peace Pledge Union for plates 79 and 80; to Oxendales for plates 23 and 107; to *The Times* for plates 128 and 129; to Associated Press Ltd for plate 1; to Burnley Public Libraries for plate 113; to Butlins for plate 63; to Chris Makepeace for plate 73; to EMI for plate 59; to Fox Photos for plate 60; to the International Brigade Association for plate 83; to the Mander & Mitchenson Collection for plate 11; to the Mansell Collection for plate 57; to National Council of Social Service for plate 46; to National Trust for plate 49; to Nelson Central Library for plate 36; to Ronald Proctor for plate 82; to H. Sargeant for plate 119 and to Sport & General for plate 95. No copyright has been wittingly infringed in any picture reproduced in this book.

PICTUREFILE

First published 1976 by Eyre Methuen Ltd   ISBN 413 32990 9
11 New Fetter Lane, EC4P 4EE
© 1976 Julian Symons
Printed in Great Britain by Hazell Watson & Viney Ltd, Aylesbury, Bucks

A TIME OF MARCHES

When you look at some of the photographs in this book, it is easy to see why the Thirties was the angry decade of this century, a time of marches and protests. The misery of slum houses, the wretchedness of men unemployed for years and often without hope of work, the indifference of government—that is what the Thirties meant for many people.

The worst thing about unemployment was its permanence. It was not merely that years of poverty had to be endured, but that there seemed no reason why they should not go on for ever. With the poverty went humiliation. The examinations carried out by the Unemployment Assistance Board made their officials universally hated. It is difficult in the Seventies to imagine what life was like in the Thirties for the tenth of the population at the bottom of the income scale. Today there is moonlighting, there is the Lump, there are forty ways of working fiddles to avoid declaring your total income for taxation. To understand the Thirties, you have to realise that then there were six people for every job, so that an employer could pick and choose among them, and that there was always somebody who would do the same work for a little less money. It is not condoning the evils of the present to say that this was an intolerable past.

Nobody writes impartially, but I have tried not to exaggerate. The myth that the national economy remained in the doldrums throughout the period has been thoroughly disproved. Noreen Branson and Margot Heinemann's valuable study *Britain in the Nineteen Thirties*, to which I owe a debt for some factual details, shows clearly the slow but continuous recovery of the economy from the worst of the Depression, 1931 and 1932. The condition demanded by this recovery, however, was a constant pool of unemployed. Once the government had rejected the idea of getting out of the Depression by the expansionist methods

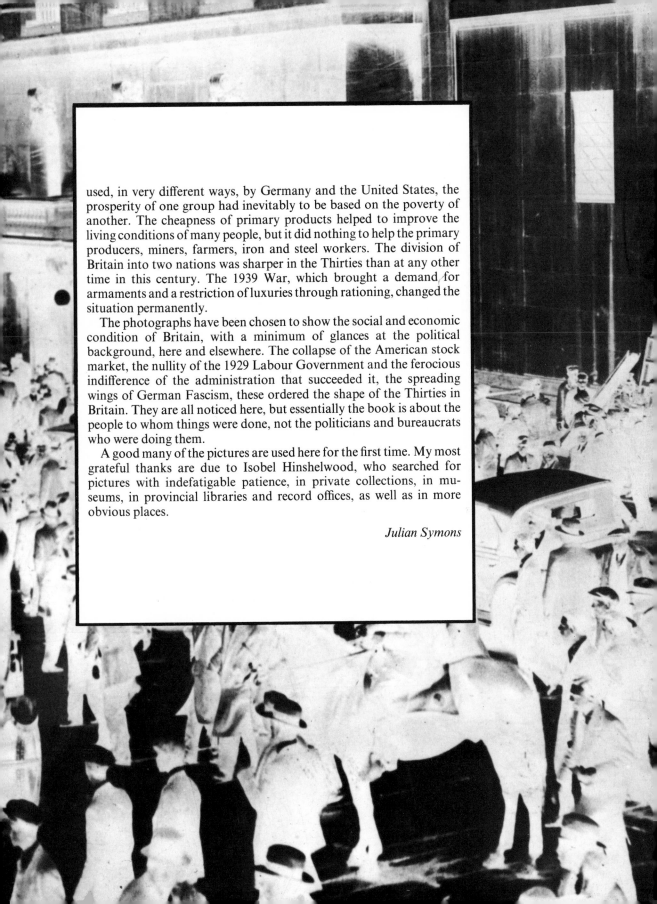

used, in very different ways, by Germany and the United States, the prosperity of one group had inevitably to be based on the poverty of another. The cheapness of primary products helped to improve the living conditions of many people, but it did nothing to help the primary producers, miners, farmers, iron and steel workers. The division of Britain into two nations was sharper in the Thirties than at any other time in this century. The 1939 War, which brought a demand for armaments and a restriction of luxuries through rationing, changed the situation permanently.

The photographs have been chosen to show the social and economic condition of Britain, with a minimum of glances at the political background, here and elsewhere. The collapse of the American stock market, the nullity of the 1929 Labour Government and the ferocious indifference of the administration that succeeded it, the spreading wings of German Fascism, these ordered the shape of the Thirties in Britain. They are all noticed here, but essentially the book is about the people to whom things were done, not the politicians and bureaucrats who were doing them.

A good many of the pictures are used here for the first time. My most grateful thanks are due to Isobel Hinshelwood, who searched for pictures with indefatigable patience, in private collections, in museums, in provincial libraries and record offices, as well as in more obvious places.

Julian Symons

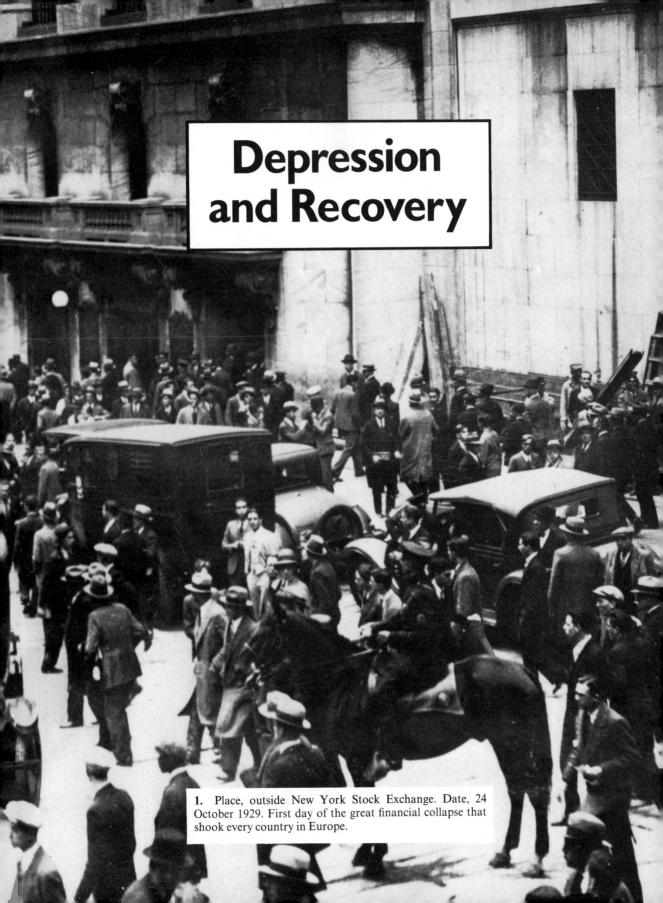

Depression and Recovery

1. Place, outside New York Stock Exchange. Date, 24 October 1929. First day of the great financial collapse that shook every country in Europe.

2.3. June, 1929. The second Labour Government takes office, full of optimism. In front Ramsay MacDonald (Prime Minister), Arthur Henderson (Foreign Secretary), Sidney Webb now Lord Parmoor (Lord President of the Council). Behind Tom Shaw (War), Arthur Greenwood (Health), Noel Buxton (Agriculture). Outside the Cabinet is Sir Oswald Mosley, the brightest spark in a Government far from dazzling. He is Chancellor of the Duchy of Lancaster.

4–7. The Labour Government had been put into office in the belief that it could solve the unemployment problem. This it dramatically failed to do. The numbers rose and rose until in August, 1931, they were 2,700,000. The American earthquake had made every financial structure shaky. Should the Government restrict or expand? In practice they dithered. Work was stopped on Cunarder 534 because of "unprecedented world conditions". The airship R101 crashed on a trial trip in October, 1930. Nearly fifty people died, including the Air Minister and the Director of Civil Aviation. In September, 1931 there was a revolt in the Atlantic Fleet at Invergordon—the first for more than a century—in protest at pay reductions that affected the men much more than the officers.

NAVY SENSATION: UNREST AMONG MEN

ATLANTIC FLEET RECALLED

Manoeuvres Suspended by Admiralty for Investigation Into Grievances

... SEQUEL TO CUTS IN PAY

THE DAILY MIRROR, Wednesday, Sept. 16, 1931.

...ed last night by the

NAVAL SENSATION—PAGE 3

...VALUE

Mr. C. W. Fane and Miss Pauline Margaret Mackie, daughter of the Bishop of Grantham, leaving Lincoln Cathedral yesterday after their wedding, the first to take place in the cathedral for thirty-one years.

Admiral Sir Mic...

Daily Mirror

THE DAILY PICTURE NEWSPAPER WITH THE LARGEST NET SALE

No. 8,680   Registered at the G.P.O. as a Newspaper.   WEDNESDAY, SEPTEMBER 16, 1931   One Penny

SIR J.
FOR

Staunch F
Confessi

ELECT

Sir John Sin
ber for Spen
Free Trader.
In favour of
Speaking u
mous. Sir Jo'
We had ar
from abroad
He had
there wou
Whatever
circumsta
the temp

The
it had
export
be tr
I t
expend
partic
a ne
m
t
I

UNREST IN THE NAVY:

Full Wireless on Page 14

EXERCISES SUSPENDED FOR PAY CUTS INVESTIGATION

Rear-Admiral Wilfred Tomkinson, who was posted Rear-Admiral Commanding Battle-Cruiser Squadron last April.

A painting party in the Atlantic Fleet battleship Rodney.

The battle-cruiser Hood, in which Rear-Admiral Tomkinson is flying his flag.

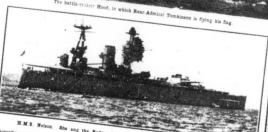

H.M.S. Nelson. She and the Rodney have a crew of 1,314 when carrying full complement.

Destroyers of the Atlantic Fleet passing the Forth Bridge on their way to commence the manoeuvres which have been suspended.

According to a statement issued yesterday by the Admiralty, the senior officer of the Atlantic Fleet, Rear-Admiral Wilfred Tomkinson, has reported that the promulgation of the reduced rates in naval pay has led to unrest amongst a proportion of the lower ratings. In consequence he has deemed it desirable to suspend the Fleet exercises while representations of the hardships occasioned by certain of the cuts are investigated in order that they may be reported for consideration by the Board of the Admiralty.

T
is
an
ief
ued
the
these
ain of
pay
certain.

T
achine in
will d
ed record
for him to

The Daily Herald

High Water London Bridge 5.8 a.m. : 5.46 p.m.

WHAT IS THE EMPIRE CRUSADE?
by
LORD BEAVERBROOK

Lord Beaverbrook

THE Empire Crusade is a movement inspired by a great ideal and advocating a practical policy.

The idea is the welding of the countries of the Empire into an economic unit which shall be the most powerful and richest group of nations on earth.

The policy is first to break down so far as possible the tariff walls which now divide the different members of the British Commonwealth, so that trade can flow between them without hindrance; and second to give adequate protection to all the producers of the Empire, whether industrial or agricultural, by imposing a duty on imports from foreign countries.

The British Empire is potentially the greatest producer of wealth that the world has ever known. It covers a quarter of the earth's surface and contains a quarter of its population. Every variety of climate and of soil is to be found within its frontiers. Yet at the present time it is largely dependent on foreign sources of supply for its necessary requirements.

The foodstuffs that we need in this country could all be raised either on our own soil or in the British Dominions, Colonies and Protectorates.

The coal, machinery and textiles that the increasing populations of our new territories overseas demand, could be supplied by the mines and factories of Great Britain and its dominions.

We ask, therefore, that the producers of the Empire should co-operate to supply each other's needs. We believe that they can do

so. We believe that if only they are given the opportunity, they will seize it and achieve a measure of prosperity which under our present fiscal system is unimaginable.

With the regular markets and increased demand which Empire Free Trade would create, unemployment would drop, costs of production both for manufacturers, and farmers would be reduced, and there would be a corresponding decrease in the price level and in taxation.

This movement is political, but it is the property of no political party.

It appeals to every man and woman in Great Britain, whatever their previous inclinations, to join in working for a great idea, which, once it is realised, will mean to each one of them a higher and a better standard of life than they can enjoy to-day.

I have stated this new policy in a manifesto which is published to-day, and I invite all those who believe that prosperity can only be achieved on Imperial lines to obtain and read a copy forthwith.

8.9. The Labour Government broke on the expansion or restriction argument. Mosley's expansionist memorandum, which suggested a big programme of public works, was rejected. He resigned, and founded the short-lived New Party. Restriction won, with cuts all round, including one of 10% in unemployment pay. This split the Labour Party. MacDonald resigned, and returned to head a National Government. At a General Election in October, 1931, their majority was 502. Labour lost over 200 seats. The picture shows the new Cabinet in the garden of 10, Downing Street. The restrictionist Socialist Chancellor, Philip Snowdon, is on the right.

Many nostrums were suggested for ailing Britain. One was Lord Beaverbrook's Empire Crusade, which he pursued throughout the decade. He ran some Parliamentary candidates, with little success.

10.   September, 1931. The Nazis have won power in the
Thuringian Government, and Hitler celebrates. Their supremacy in Germany is eighteen months ahead.

11. July, 1934. Mosley, now leader of the British Union of Fascists, holds one of his biggest—and rowdiest—meetings, at Olympia.

Daily Herald

No. 4956 • MONDAY, JANUARY 4, 1932 • ONE PENNY

OUR GIGANTIC NEW FREE INSURANCE

SICKNESS BENEFITS: EDUCATION GRANTS FOR CHILDREN: SPECIAL BOUNTIES FOR TWINS

Railway	Education Grants	Sickness Benefit
£20,000	£100	£10-10-0
Steamer—Bus—Tram—Chara-banc—Passenger Lift, etc.	*Sports—Boating and Bathing —Flying*	*Home Accidents*
£1,000	£500	£200
All Fatal Accidents	*Bounty for Twins*	*Cycling and Motor-cycling*
£100	£5-5-0	£100
Street Accidents	*Private Road Conveyances*	*Accidents to Scouts, Guides, etc.* *Children*
£200	£200	£10 £3

Gandhi Arrested In Bed On Terrace At 3 a.m.

MR. GANDHI

IN JAIL WITH MR. V. PATEL

Police Plan To Seize Mahatma On Train Foiled

MR. V. PATEL

PICCAVER MISSING AFTER AIR CRASH HOAX

MR. ALFRED PICCAVER, the famous operatic tenor, who left England in his early manhood, found success in Vienna, and was to have returned to his native land to sing at the London Palladium to-night, is missing.

Because of an economy cut at the Vienna State Opera House, which would have reduced his salary by £30 for each performance, Mr. Piccaver severed his connection with Austria, and decided to come to London.

He was expected at Victoria yesterday afternoon by the boat train arriving at 4.42.

A crowd of admirers, including representatives of the Austrian colony in London, and an elderly man from Long Sutton, Lincs., Piccaver's native town, gathered to welcome him. He was not on the train.

Three later trains were met by his impresario, Mr. Henry Sherek, a representative of the London Palladium, and a dwindling crowd of enthusiasts. He was not on any of them.

Up to midnight no word had been received from him as to his whereabouts, or whether he had made any change of plans.

AIR ACCIDENT MYTH

"Mr. Piccaver's manager told me by telephone on Thursday that the singer would leave Vienna at 2 p.m. and, travelling via Ostend, reach Victoria this afternoon, said Mr. Sherek to the "Daily Herald," last night.

"Since then I have heard nothing. He is due to sing at the Palladium to-morrow evening, and I am getting anxious.

"At one period of the evening I received a telephone message purporting to come from Brussels, which said that he was flying to London and was forced down at Ostend. This turned out to be a hoax."

Piccaver, although an Englishman by real name is Alfred Peckover—has only sung twice in his native country.

To-DAY WE ARE PROUD TO PUT BEFORE OUR READERS AND, THROUGH THEM, TO THE FAR GREATER NUMBER OF THEIR DEPENDENTS, OUR AMAZING 1932 FREE INSURANCE OFFER FOR WHICH MILLIONS HAVE BEEN WAITING.

The announcement you now read automatically confers on the homes of all our registered readers a Security wider and more generous than has ever before been offered.

And it offers the same inestimable boon to every person in the land, irrespective of sex, or station, or any other distinction, at the mere stroke of the pen.

ALL FATAL ACCIDENTS

Greatly increased Travel Benefits, Education Grants for children who have lost their bread-winners, cover against ALL Fatal Accidents, Sickness Benefits, Bounties for Twins and new protection for ever-active Youth stand out conspicuously.

We give above a selection of the impressive array of benefits which, even if they stood alone, would protect you and all who depend on you in countless different directions.

But they are not all. Very far from it. They are but a few of the items of our greatly extended scheme, but they provide you with the main outlines of our remarkable offer.

TURN TO PAGE TEN

To realise the unsurpassed generosity of our 1932 Scheme, you have only to turn to Page Ten, where you will find the Benefits and Conditions in full.

One of the first decisions we made when planning our 1932 offer was to produce the perfect Free Family Insurance.

We think our readers will agree that we have been highly successful and that we have established a new standard unparalleled in newspaper insurance enterprise.

£20,000 RAILWAY BENEFIT

This important Benefit is doubled at a stroke. Our Free Railway Insurance is increased from £10,000 to £20,000.

£100 EDUCATION GRANTS

One of the greatest tragedies of life is when a child is taken away from the school it has grown to love because the bread-winner has been killed. For this reason the "Daily Herald" has decided to make a special provision of Education Grants up to £100 for the child or children up to the ages of 17 of Registered Readers where the life of the bread-winner is lost through a fatal accident.

SICKNESS BENEFITS

No home is immune from the ever-present menace of Sickness. The "Daily Herald" has planned on generous lines an Insurance against

---

certain serious illnesses which will appeal to all our readers and provide a very substantial aid to paying Doctor's Bills and to making possible the very necessary sick-room luxuries.

BOUNTIES FOR TWINS.

Twins, though they are a present of which to be proud, bring with them greatly increased expenses. For this reason the "Daily Herald" is offering a special Bounty of £5 5s. 5d. for Twins.

£10 FOR SCOUTS, GUIDES, ETC.

Children who belong to Scouts, Guides and recognised Organisations of Youth are entitled under the new "Daily Herald" Scheme to a special Accident Benefit of £10. For Scout Masters, Guide Mistresses and those in charge of Youth Organisations a similar Benefit is provided.

There are also benefits for injuries sustained in steamers, buses, trams, taxis, motor-coaches, passenger lifts, or private vehicles, benefits in respect of Cycling and Motor-Cycling accidents, Sports accidents, Home accidents, and accidents to the Children.

PENSIONS FOR LIFE

And last, but by no means least, there is a pension of up to £6 per week for life in the event of permanent total disablement in Travel accidents.

Everyone takes risks when travelling. No worker is free from the dangers of the factory. Mothers at home, fathers in their gardens, husbands and wives in their family cars, grown-up or children in their sports, bathers, cyclists, motor-cyclists, children at their games—all are in immediate need of the boons of the unparalleled "Daily Herald" scheme.

Think of this wonderful Gift, and remember that the "Daily Herald" offers it to you Free. It is a luxury you owe your family to Register without delay.

NO NEED TO RE-REGISTER

If you are already a Registered Reader, you are automatically qualified for the full range of Benefits now published, and there is no need to re-register unless you have changed your address or your newsagent.

If you are not already registered, spend two minutes more wisely than you have ever done before by turning to Page Ten and filling in the Forms without delay. One registration covers Husband, Wife and Children (between the ages of 6 and 15).

There were 7,583 families who benefited under our Scheme in 1931. You never know when you, too, may be glad of the help which the "Daily Herald" offers you Free.

Only a stroke of the Pen is needed.

DO IT NOW

All Benefits in the Greatly Extended "Daily Herald" 1932 Free Insurance announced to-day are retrospective to 6 a.m., January 1st, 1932.

[Leading Article on Page Eight]

MR. W. GRAHAM GRAVELY ILL

PNEUMONIA AFTER INFLUENZA

MR. WILLIAM GRAHAM, former Labour M.P. for Edinburgh Central, and President of the Board of Trade in the last Labour Government, is lying gravely ill at his Hendon home.

He is suffering from acute lobar pneumonia, which affects the whole of the lungs at once.

Dr. A. [...] and his colleague [...]

THE Government of India has struck. Soon after three o'clock this morning Mr. Gandhi was arrested in bed and taken to Yerwada Jail, near Poona.

His arrest is under the terms of the Bombay Ordinance of 1827—which means that he will be kept in prison without being brought to trial or charged with any definite offence.

Mr. Vallabhai Patel, President of the Indian National Congress, was arrested at the same time and also taken to Yerwada.

Mr. Subhas Bose, the young Left-Wing leader, who has been Mayor of Calcutta, had already been arrested on Saturday on his way to confer with Mr. Gandhi at Bombay.

It is now expected that the whole Congress organisation [...] will follow.

Mule Singh, [...] he gained his third title of the tournament.

In to-day's singles tournament Perry opened cautiously and seemed to be tiring Borotra. Borotra showed some magnificent form in the early part of the match, but soon became exhausted, and Perry was able to force him to accept his style of game.

VERY MILD

(See Page Three)

	PAGE
Woman's World	5
Commander Kenworthy on Labour's United Voice	6
What Women Can't Do! by Gilbert Frankau; Gadfly; Gossip	7
Serial and Letters	12
F. L. Mannock's Film Notes and Radio	13

Mr. Gandhi an interview.

I understand that the Governor of Bombay, Sir Frederick Sykes, conveyed to the Viceroy such requests from the local European Chamber of Commerce and the European Association.

Sir Tej Bahadur Sapru and Mr. Jayakar, the moderate leaders of Indian opinion, had also been in communication with the Viceroy.

Mr. Jayakar had a long conversation with Mr. Gandhi during the afternoon. He told me that he found Mr. Gandhi extremely reasonable, and doing his best.

Mr. Gandhi sent a message to Sir Tej saying that the march of events had overpowered him, but that the door of negotiation, so far as he was concerned, was still open.

One compromise suggested was that Sir James Crerar, the Home Member of the Viceroy's Council, should meet Mr. Gandhi in Bombay.

HIS LAST PURCHASE

One of Mr. Gandhi's last acts in preparing for his departure (adds Reuter) was to buy two watches for presentation to the two Scotland Yard detectives, Sergeant William Evans and Sergeant William Rogers, who were his bodyguard in Europe.

Swiss watches were chosen by his secretary, but he insisted on the best English levers. When it was pointed out that this was inconsistent with the boycott resolution, he said: "When I made the promise to give them watches the Delhi truce was still in force, and the boycott resolution, therefore, does not

(Continued on Page Two)

12–16. The newspaper circulation war of the early Thirties produced extraordinary offers to registered readers, like the one shown here. But travel insurance and education grants meant little to the army of unemployed, who sang in hope of supper, carried sandwich boards, or collected pebbles for which they received 6/– a ton.

Gandhi being welcomed in London a year before his arrest in India.

I KNOW 3 TRADES
I SPEAK 3 LANGUAGES
FOUGHT FOR 3 YEARS
HAVE 3 CHILDREN
AND NO WORK FOR
3 MONTHS
BUT I ONLY WANT
ONE JOB

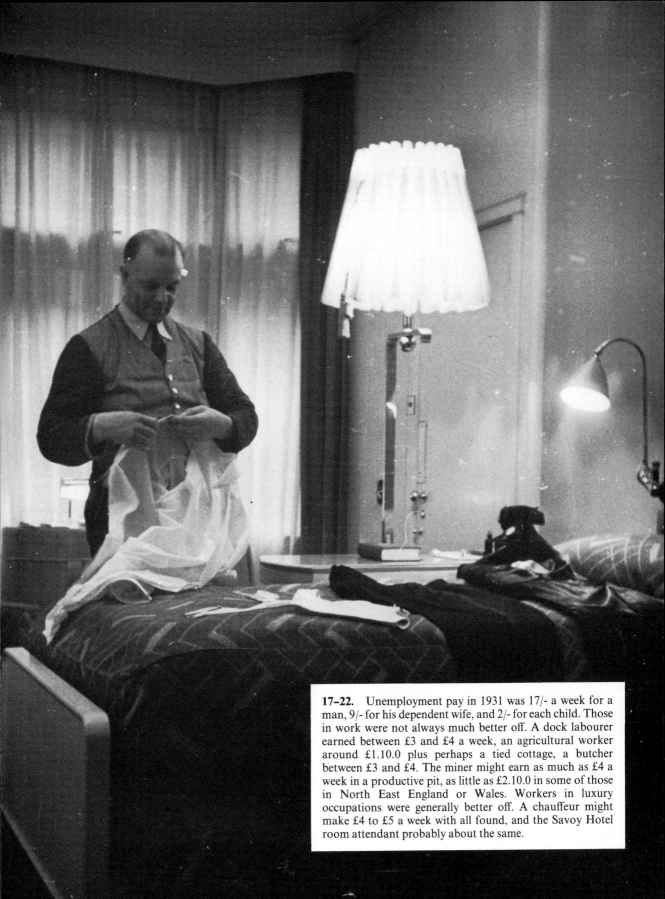

17–22. Unemployment pay in 1931 was 17/- a week for a man, 9/- for his dependent wife, and 2/- for each child. Those in work were not always much better off. A dock labourer earned between £3 and £4 a week, an agricultural worker around £1.10.0 plus perhaps a tied cottage, a butcher between £3 and £4. The miner might earn as much as £4 a week in a productive pit, as little as £2.10.0 in some of those in North East England or Wales. Workers in luxury occupations were generally better off. A chauffeur might make £4 to £5 a week with all found, and the Savoy Hotel room attendant probably about the same.

Five Extraordinary Summer Bargains!

The finest Bargains in the whole Catalogue! Here they are—five of the most attractive Frocks you ever have seen at anywhere near these prices. For Frocks which are splendidly made—in fine materials—Frocks you will wear with distinct pleasure—this page offers you the best opportunity!

Model O 4494—A Washing Frock that is both dressy and smart carried out in a soft gleaming Artificial Silk exactly like Crêpe-de-Chine in appearance, the style exceedingly graceful and refined-looking, entirely in one shade with the right trimming note introduced by the pretty collar of Guipure lace and tiny fancy buttons on the front of Dress and on the banded cuffs. The bodice is effectively styled with tiny pin-tucks in panel effect, the skirt gracefully full with wide box-pleat at each side, and finished all-round belt of the self material, tying with long flowing ends. Shades : Ivory, Peach, Eau de Nil, Beige, Old-rose, Princess-blue.

Oxendale's Price only 14/11

O.S., 39 to 45 ins. bust	...	3/- extra.
X.O.S., over 45 ins. bust	...	6/- ,,
Over 44 ins. long	...	2/- ,,

Model O 4498—A very special Bargain indeed. Such a dainty and attractive little Frock of fine, soft, Artificial Silk Crêpe de Chine—just perfectly made in a style so chic with the new long pointed bodice effect and a full width circular skirt. Rows of fine pin tucks trim the bodice in harmony with the pointed hip piping, the dainty Collar of contrasting colour neatly piped and finished long tie ends, the cuffs of the sleeves in contrast to match. Neat stitching on the all-round Belt matches the pin-tuck trimming, and the skirt is most beautifully styled with centre inverted pleat, and, think of it, only 12/11. Shades : Princess-blue, Biskra, New Brown, Sandal, Almond-green, Navy, All-Black.

Oxendale's Price only 12/11

O.S., 39 to 45 ins. bust	...	3/- extra.
X.O.S., over 45 ins. bust	...	6/- ,,
Over 44 ins. long	...	2/- ,,

O 4494

O 4498

Model O 4495

(On Right).

You'll be charmed with the exquisitely pretty pattern of this choice new Figured Voile—so tastefully smart and attractive in soft contrasting colours, made on free-fitting graceful lines with Robespierre collar of White Organdi Muslin, edged in dainty lace, the full-length sleeves having smart turn-back cuffs trimmed with the same lace ; the skirt, as you see, is a quite new style, so charming in a soft, fluttery Voile, the Overskirt of large scalloped outline edged with stitching in colour to match the design. Shades predominating : Lemon/Flame, Jade/Cedar, Rose/Cedar, Saxe/Cedar Brown/Cedar, and Lido/Rose.

Oxendale's Price only 12/11

		Extra.
O.S., 39 to 45 ins. bust ...	...	3/-
X.O.S., over 45 ins. bust ...	...	6/-
Over 44 ins. long...	...	2/-

O 4495

O 4496

O 4497

Model O 4496—As a House Frock or for Walking Out, this neat and serviceable style is a thoroughly practical Frock which will do splendid service in constant wear. Made on latest lines in a fine Washing Poplin of very strong quality, it is a Frock of really nice dressy appearance, the bodice neatly pin-tucked and with the favourite rever collar, trimmed in Beige Poplin with tie to match ; the useful full-length sleeves having turn-back cuffs of the Beige material, too, the skirt pleasingly full with wide pleats at each side stitched down to give the stylish hip-yoke effect, and all-round belt showing a neat buckle. Shades : White, Sky, Nil, Apple-green, Dark Saxe, New Brown, Peach, and Wine.

Oxendale's Price only 7/6

O.S., 39 to 45 ins. bust,	2/6 extra.	
X.O.S., over 45 ins. bust,	5/- ,,	
Over 44 ins. long	... 1/6 ,,	

Model O 4497

(On Left).

New in design and beautifully made, this dainty and smart Frock is ever so pretty, the charming pattern in tasteful colours, very neat and yet quite attractively suited for Summer-day wear. A graceful and becoming Frock on latest lines in a strong, finely woven figured Washing fabric, the style features the becoming Robespierre collar, bound plain colour to tone with floating ends, the turn-back cuffs showing the same effective trimming, while pin-tucking on the bodice indicates the line of the pleats giving such charming fullness to the skirt, which has a loosely-fitting belt of self material. Shades : Jade/Beige, Cedar/Beige, Moonlight/Beige, Red/Navy/Beige, Navy/Saxe/Beige.

Oxendale's Price only 7/6

O.S., 39 to 45 ins. bust, 2/6 extra.		
X.O.S., over 45 ins. bust, 5/- ,,		
Over 44 ins. long	... 1/6 ,,	

Prices

23–25. If you relate earnings to prices, the picture looks better. The page from a mail order catalogue shows that it was possible to dress cheaply, and Woolworth really did contain articles that cost only sixpence. The shop prices on page 20 are staggering—choice red salmon at 1/- a tin, and corned beef at 8½d. For between £15 and £30 down, and £1 a week, you could buy one of those semi-detached suburban houses that are said to be the Englishman's dream. Yet the real point is that for many families these houses were as unattainable as Buckingham Palace. What chance had a man with a family, earning £3 a week, got of paying £1 a week mortgage?

26. Hulme, Lancashire, in 1933. The glass-fronted case is only 10/6, the desk in the background 21/-. And Craven A, like most cigarettes, were 10 for 6d.

Housing

27–29. If you tried to find the most potent reason for anger in the Thirties, it might be housing policy. It was the decade of private building for middle-class and lower-middle-class salaried workers, the time of ribbon development and the joyful destruction of the countryside. It was also the decade when, in spite of frequent expression of horror at the existence of slums, little was done to clear them. By the time the War came there was no real shortage of houses in Britain, only a shortage of people who could afford to live in them. The pictures show a street scene from the film "Housing Problems", made for the Gas Corporation in 1935, and typical slum exteriors in Birmingham and (right) Liverpool.

30-33. The contrasts offered are obvious enough, but they do suggest a real division of Britain into two societies, less of rich and poor than of one world in which it was necessary above all to be respectable, and another in which it was difficult even to remain clean. Angelina Street in Birmingham (bottom-right) is typical in its dinginess, and the interior (left), with the wireless cabinet having pride of place, is typical too. The semi-detached suburban dream needed a car for its fulfilment. The ownership of a car was very much (to use a term then unknown) a status symbol. Another still from "Housing Problems" shows a back view of terraced houses, a jumble of roofs, washing, broken-down shanty outhouses.

34–35. The slum bed-sitting room is in Gower Street, Liverpool, about 1933. Two small gas mantles (one reflected in the mirror) provide the only illumination. About the other picture there is an air of ineffable complacency.

36–37. The Nelson Harmonic Club is taking children on a day's outing. For the working and lower-middle-class the railway retained its supremacy as a means of travel. Summer holidays were taken in Britain, at seaside towns into which you were decanted from a train. Picnic outings in cars were the mark, again, of those with a different position in society.

Protest

38–40. At Gresford Colliery, North Wales, there was a pit explosion in September, 1934, through which 264 men died. It was the worst mining disaster for more than twenty years. The Commission of Inquiry which reported $2\frac{1}{2}$ years later, severely censured the Colliery management for ignoring safety precautions. No disciplinary action, however, was taken against the censured inspectors.

On the left, unemployed South Wales workers marching on London in 1932. On the right, unemployed Manchester women in a protest march.

41. An unemployed demonstration in Bristol in 1932, which started off with a strike of newsboys, developed a few days later into a two hour street battle. There were several police baton charges. Thirty people were taken to hospital.

42–45. On the left, members of the British Union of Fascists, standing by their lorries at Chelsea HQ, ready for action. Below, a Nazi youth parade in 1932, still before Hitler reached power. On the right, Mussolini greets the doddering Ramsay MacDonald in 1933, as the Prime Minister lands at Ostia from a seaplane for talks on—disarmament. MacDonald found in the dictator's ideas on peace "a wonderful similarity to my own". In the same year, the trial in Moscow of six Metropolitan-Vickers engineers on spying charges caused a crisis in Anglo-Russian relations. Three were expelled, the others given prison sentences. A British trade ban followed, but the embargo was raised after a few months when the engineers were set free.

46–48. The new Police College at Hendon was opened in May, 1934 by the Prince of Wales. The intention was to recruit more intelligent and better educated officers, but the attempt to create an elite met with strong opposition. The picture shows cadets receiving instruction. Below, Yarmouth fishermen idle during a strike. Above, a still from Paul Rotha's *Today We Live*, showing a decaying industrial site in South Wales.

Recovery

49–51. The upturn in the economy which began in the middle Thirties continued until the War. It was associated with the American recovery, and with the development of new and sometimes luxury industries. The improvement in living conditions for those in work was slight but real. By 1938 the average wage of agricultural labourers had gone up from approximately £1.10.0 a week to £1.15.0. Sugar beet (left) was developed successfully during the decade. And something was done, through the National Trust, to check the spoliation of the countryside. Montacute House, near Yeovil, was bought by the Trust in 1931.

52–55. Testing small Electrolux refrigerators; producing a luxury item, toy cars; finishing off bicycles in a Birmingham plant; an automatic spooling machine in use at British Thread Mills, Leicester.

56. *following pages.* Upholstering and trimming Morris car bodies at Cowley. The number of private cars doubled during the Thirties.

57-58. Kinlochleven Hydro electric works, with the village seen from the pipeline; and Piccadilly Circus all lit up, with Eros barely visible.

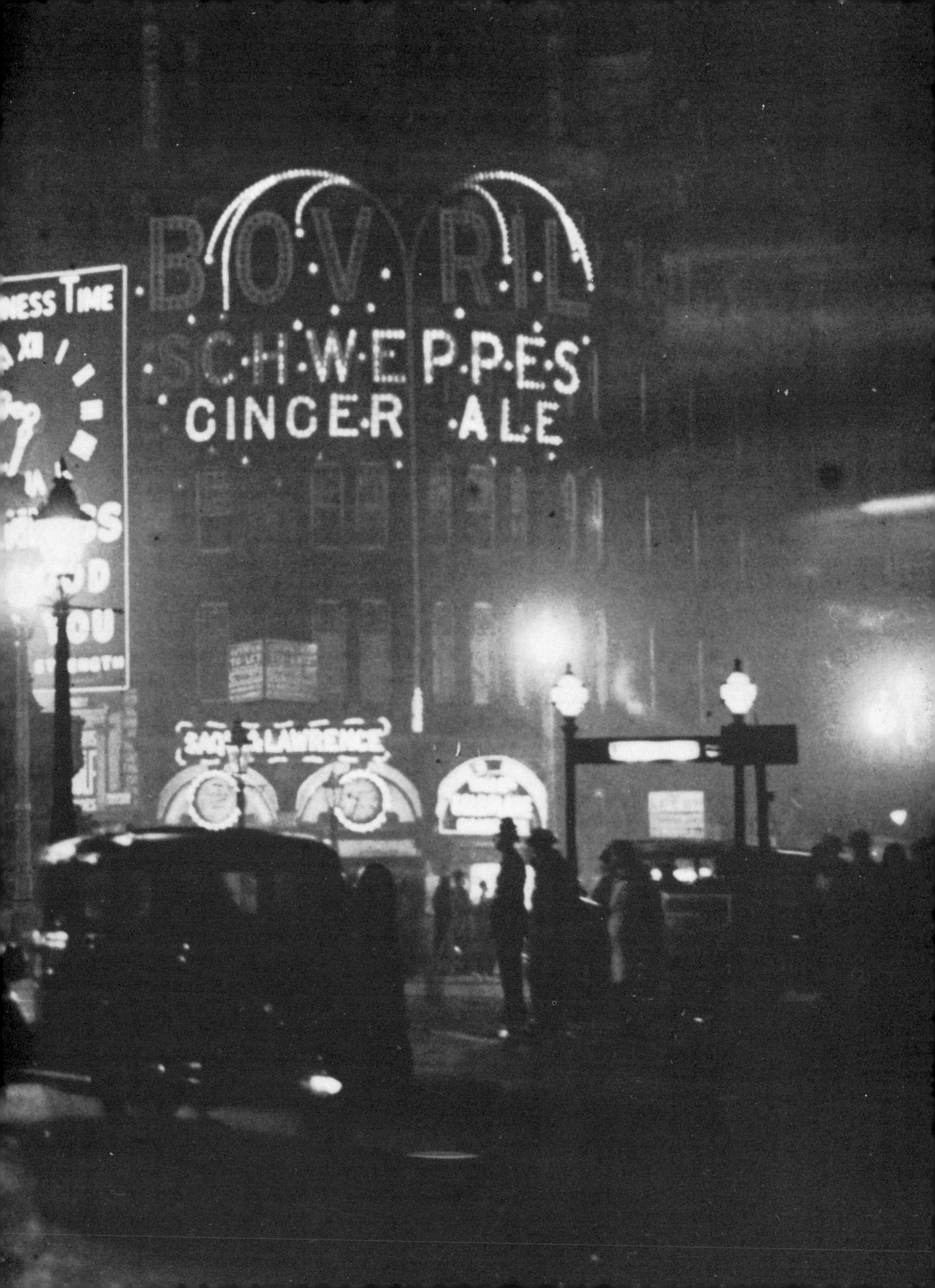
BOVRIL
SCHWEPPES
GINGER ALE

59–61. The British film industry flourished briefly in the first half of the decade. Anthony Asquith, crouched on the front of the hansom cab, is directing Ann Casson and Carl Harbord in "Dance, Pretty Lady" (1931), made from Compton Mackenzie's *Carnival*. On the right the Cheltenham Flyer, breaker of records, and the first train to travel regularly at over 70 mph. Above, listening to the wireless with headphones, a refinement no longer available to train passengers.

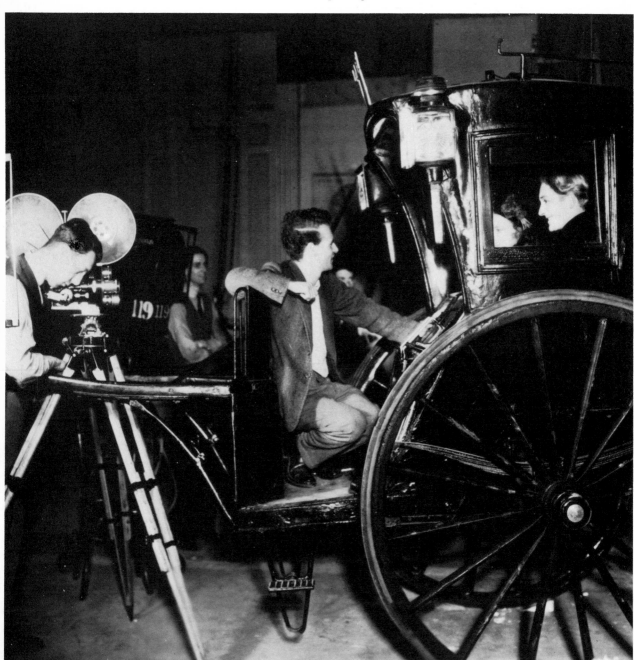

Seeing it Through with STRUBE

Sidney Strube, the *Daily Express* cartoonist, was not internationally famous like David Low, yet in some ways he gives a clearer idea of national feeling during the decade. His hero is the Little Man of a thousand editorials, the David who knocks out Goliath Kid Slump, is suspicious of the BBC's good intentions, can't understand the new traffic regulations, is good natured although not too bright. What made Strube a great consoler was the fact that the Little Man always won through in the end. This selection of cartoons over the space of twelve months shows the Little Man seeing it through with Strube.

NOVEMBER FIGHT RESULT

December 1st, 1933.

CHORUS OF FOREIGN CHAMPIONS: " How is it you can do that and we can't? "
THE LITTLE CHAMPION: " Why, it's just an old British custom! "

December 2nd, 1933.

" Don't forget we're swotting hard to get our college ' blues.'
Play the game, you cads, play the game!
So please don't be too difficult when leaving any clues—
Play the game, you cads, pl-a-ay the game."

(With apologies to the Western Brothers.)

The reference is to the plans for Hendon Police College (see page 40). The politicians are MacDonald and J. H. Thomas. The Western Brothers were popular monocled mock upper class comics.

A comment on the different laws for the rich and the working class drinker, with a touch of xenophobia thrown in.

"SPECIAL OCCASIONS"   December 7th, 1933.

FOOD FOR THOUGHT

January 10th, 1934.

Controversy between the Ministry of Health and the British Medical Association will come before the House when Parliament meets.

5

"I WISH I HAD SOME WORK TO DO."
"SO DO I!"

February 5th, 1934.

4   INVISIBLE MENDING   *February 24th, 1934.*

THE FREEDOM OF THE B.B.C.

A national character gives a talk on free speech.

March 15th, 1934.

THE OPERA SEASON OPENS

(At the opening of the Opera Season at Covent Garden Sir Thomas Beecham severely rebuked the audience for talking during the Overture.)

May 2nd, 1934.

The conductor is Lord Beaverbrook, the Little Man is seen as Empire Crusader. Beaverbrook owned the *Daily Express*.

THE LION IN THE DANIELS' DEN

May 25th, 1934.

3

More flattery for Beaverbrook the lion.

New one way traffic systems were introduced in 1934.

More confusion for the Little Man with the spread of traffic lights.

WHAT THE STARS DID NOT FORETELL   June 27th, 1934.

England unexpectedly beat the Australians in a Test Match.

"MEN IN WHITE"   June 28th, 1934.

An operation scene will be shown in a new London play to-night.

LITTLE MAN: "WHO'S DONE ALL THIS, OFFICER?"
CONSTABLE: "—Sh—! Mr. Hore-Belisha, Sir!"
LITTLE MAN: "HORE-BELISHA?—*NEVER HEARD OF HIM!*"   September 4th, 1934.

The sounding of car horns was forbidden at night. Hore-Belisha, on left with dog, was the Minister of Transport.

The Road to War

62. By 1936 Hitler was firmly in power. His enemies were dead or in concentration camps, awkward friends and potential rivals had been killed. This piece of Left propaganda by sandwichmen catches a common feeling of menace.

Fun and Games

63. The daily physical jerks at a Butlin holiday camp in 1936. The success of these camps sprang from their cheapness and the community feeling they engendered. Holidays for workers had been based on bed-and-breakfast boarding houses. Now private chalets and communal meals replaced them, plus some regimentation. When the camp ushers called "Wakey wakey, rise and shine", you didn't stay in bed.

64–67. Nudism was a cult of the Thirties, although some retained the modesty of what was called a bathing costume. Hiking also came into favour. Groups of hikers would set off for a place by train, and start their hike from the station. The tendency towards group enjoyment was as marked here as in the success of holiday camps. All outdoor activities were regarded as healthy, and the emphasis on strenuous exercise in Soviet Russia and Nazi Germany made many people regard them favourably—surely there couldn't be much wrong with those happy singing athletes? The picture at bottom right shows women cyclists of the National Cyclists' Union at an Alexandra Park rally. At bottom left, fun for the rich or richer, in the dining room of the Queen Mary.

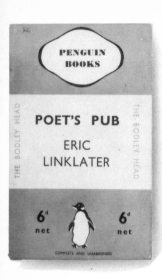

POET'S PUB

ERIC LINKLATER

MADAME CLAIRE

SUSAN ERTZ

THE UNPLEASANTNESS AT THE BELLONA CLUB

DOROTHY L. SAYERS

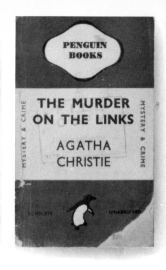

THE MURDER ON THE LINKS

AGATHA CHRISTIE

ARIEL

ANDRÉ MAUROIS

A FAREWELL TO ARMS

ERNEST HEMINGWAY

TWENTY-FIVE

BEVERLEY NICHOLS

WILLIAM

E. H. YOUNG

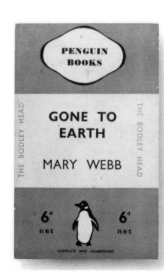

GONE TO EARTH

MARY WEBB

CARNIVAL

COMPTON MACKENZIE

Education

68–70. The first ten Penguins appeared in 1935, all priced at sixpence. Allen Lane had been told that the idea of sixpenny paperback books had no commercial future, and these first ten titles show a certain caution. The success was immense, and caution was soon abandoned. Within a couple of years a hundred books had been published, and the Pelican series been launched with Shaw's *Intelligent Woman's Guide to Socialism, Capitalism, Sovietism and Fascism*. Pelican books soon became a powerful force for political and social education, conducted from a point vaguely Left of centre, and strongly opposed to Fascism.

More orthodox education for those in state schools, which were called elementary schools, was less satisfactory. A pious official pamphlet issued in 1936 suggested that schools should be single-storey buildings, open to air and sunshine, with playgrounds well away from school buildings. Many, however, remained like this village school, with children being taught in old, unsuitable and uncomfortable buildings. Below, the wash basins in a new East London elementary school opened in 1938 by John Masefield, the Poet Laureate. The school was big for its time, providing for 870 children.

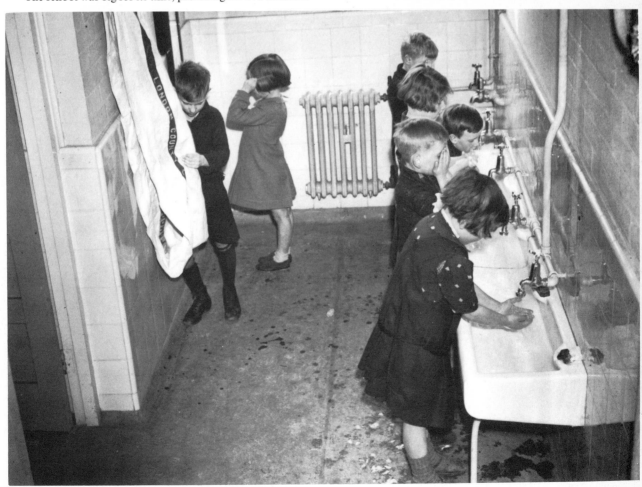

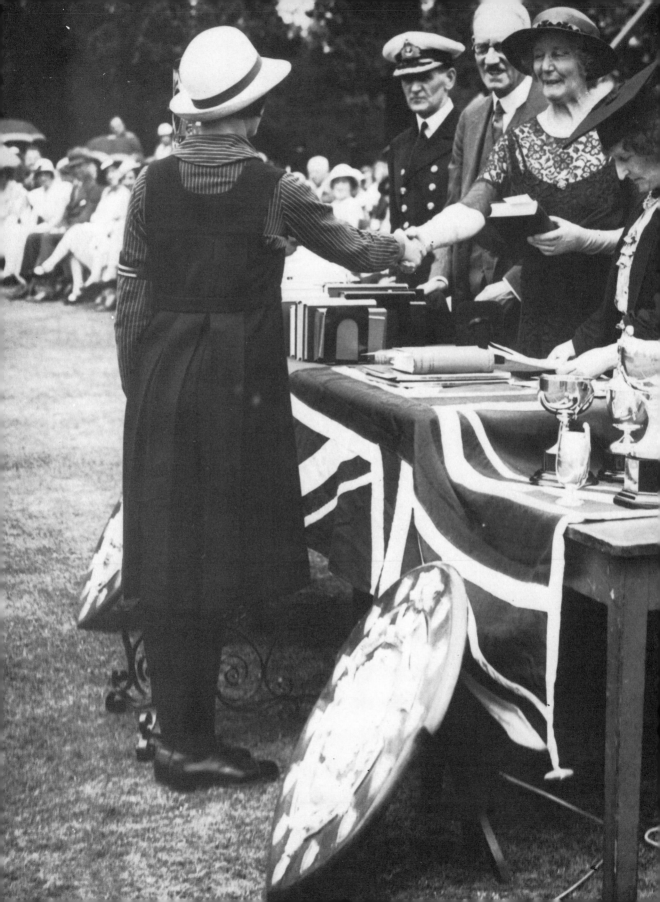

71. Prize Day at the Royal Merchant Seamen's Orphanage, Wokingham. The Good Influence prize is being awarded. Could the Lady Bountiful condescension of rich to poor be better conveyed?

Royalty

72–73. The Silver Jubilee celebrations of King George V were held in May, 1935. In January of the following year the King died, generally and genuinely mourned. The position of the English monarch was such that he was rarely included in the hatred sometimes felt for his Ministers. The King was very likely mourned even by many of the men who carried boards saying "Celebrate Jubilee Year by Finding Us Work". In 1935 the number of unemployed was still around 2,000,000, but some trades were doing well, in particular the building industry, general engineering, and car, cycle and aircraft manufacturers. Those out of work, and at the mercy of the much-hated Unemployment Assistance Board, lived as miserably as ever.

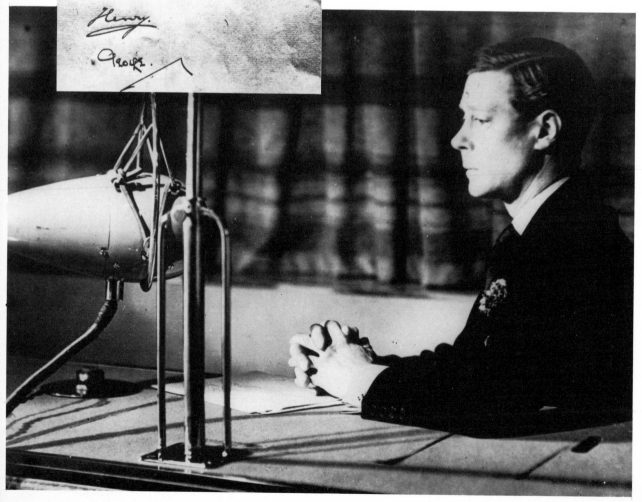

INSTRUMENT OF ABDICATION

I, Edward the Eighth, of Great Britain, Ireland, and the British Dominions beyond the Seas, King, Emperor of India, do hereby declare My irrevocable determination to renounce the Throne for Myself and for My descendants, and My desire that effect should be given to this Instrument of Abdication immediately.

In token whereof I have hereunto set My hand this tenth day of December, nineteen hundred and thirty six, in the presence of the witnesses whose signatures are subscribed.

SIGNED AT FORT BELVEDERE IN THE PRESENCE OF

Edward R I

Albert

Henry.

George.

74–76. In his farewell broadcast on 11 December, 1936 (Sir John Reith, Governor of the BBC, introduced him as "His Royal Highness Prince Edward") the former King Edward VIII said that he had always been "treated with full consideration" by his family and by Stanley Baldwin, the Prime Minister. The generally accepted view was that Baldwin's implacable opposition to marriage with a not-yet-divorced American, forced the King to abdicate. The opposition to his staying was highly organised, his support individual and sporadic. Above, the instrument of abdication, below the broadcast, opposite some feminine members of the "King's party".

MRS. SIMPSON
IN
FRANCE
LATE FINAL
STAR
ON
6.30
SIMPSON
IN FRANCE
EVENING
STANDARD
MRS.
SIMPSON
MYSTERY
6.30

CABINET'S LONG MEETING THE STAR

77-78. The Duke of Windsor and Mrs Simpson were married at the Chateau de Cande, Tours, on 3 June, 1937, almost immediately after her divorce. Later in the year the Duke visited Germany. He was now free to express his sympathy for what he regarded as the idealistic side of National Socialism, and was impressed by what he saw.

PEACE PLEDGE UNION
· DICK SHEPPARD PEACE CENTRE ·

en are Appealing
TO THE
OVERNMENTS
f the NATIONS
TO
OP THE WAR
AND TO
CUSS PEACE
you sign and
ort this appeal!

WAR
WILL CEASE
WHEN MEN
REFUSE
TO FIGHT
What are YOU going
to do about it?
THE PEACE PLEDGE UNION

THERE'S NEVER
A WRONG TIME
FOR DOING
THE RIGHT THING
★
NEGOTIATE NOW
The Peace Pledge Union
Dick Sheppard House

LABOUR
FIGHTS
WARS
and
PAYS
NEVER AGAIN

79–80. The Peace Pledge Union was basically the creation of a passionate pacifist orator, the Canon Dick Sheppard. Its simple message: "War Will Cease When Men Refuse To Fight" won the hearts of many who wanted to believe that if they refused to fight, other people would become pacifists too. By 1937 the Union had 133,000 members organised into 725 groups. Only a small proportion of them remained pacifists when the War came.

TAE. BOROUGH. SE.

81. In November, 1936, the wearing of political uniform was banned. Meetings, however, were still held, and march projected. They met with militant opposition, much of organised by the Communist Party.

Meetings, Demonstrations

82. An Oxford Group "New Enlistment" camp, Birmingham, Easter 1937. The Oxford Group (later Moral Re-Armament) made a strong appeal to people who found Dick Sheppard's pacifism too simple, but were opposed to the violent solutions of Fascism and Communism. If you looked for personal and religious, rather than political, salvation, the Oxford Group might be for you. The Group, led by a former Lutheran Minister named Frank Buchman, laid stress on Absolute Honesty and Absolute Love, and its techniques of Sharing and Guidance were strongly confessional. To those politically oriented, the Group seemed purely reactionary. During the Thirties it made some headway in Germany.

Spanish Civil War

83. The Spanish Civil War, which began in July, 1936, when General Franco rebelled against the Republican Government, prompted a great surge of sympathy for the Republican side. The British Battalion of the International Brigade, seen here, were all volunteers. Of the 2,000 British International Brigaders 500 were killed and the same number seriously wounded. Many of the rest returned disillusioned by Communist dictatorship in Spain.

84–85. A sympathy march in London, and the sinking of a British merchant steamer bombed by the rebels of Alicante. The official British "non-intervention" policy was not changed by such bombings.

86. Scots fisher girls on strike. The number of days lost through strikes increased in the later Thirties. Few strikes involved large groups of workers but some industries, like fishing and agriculture, remained depressed throughout the decade.

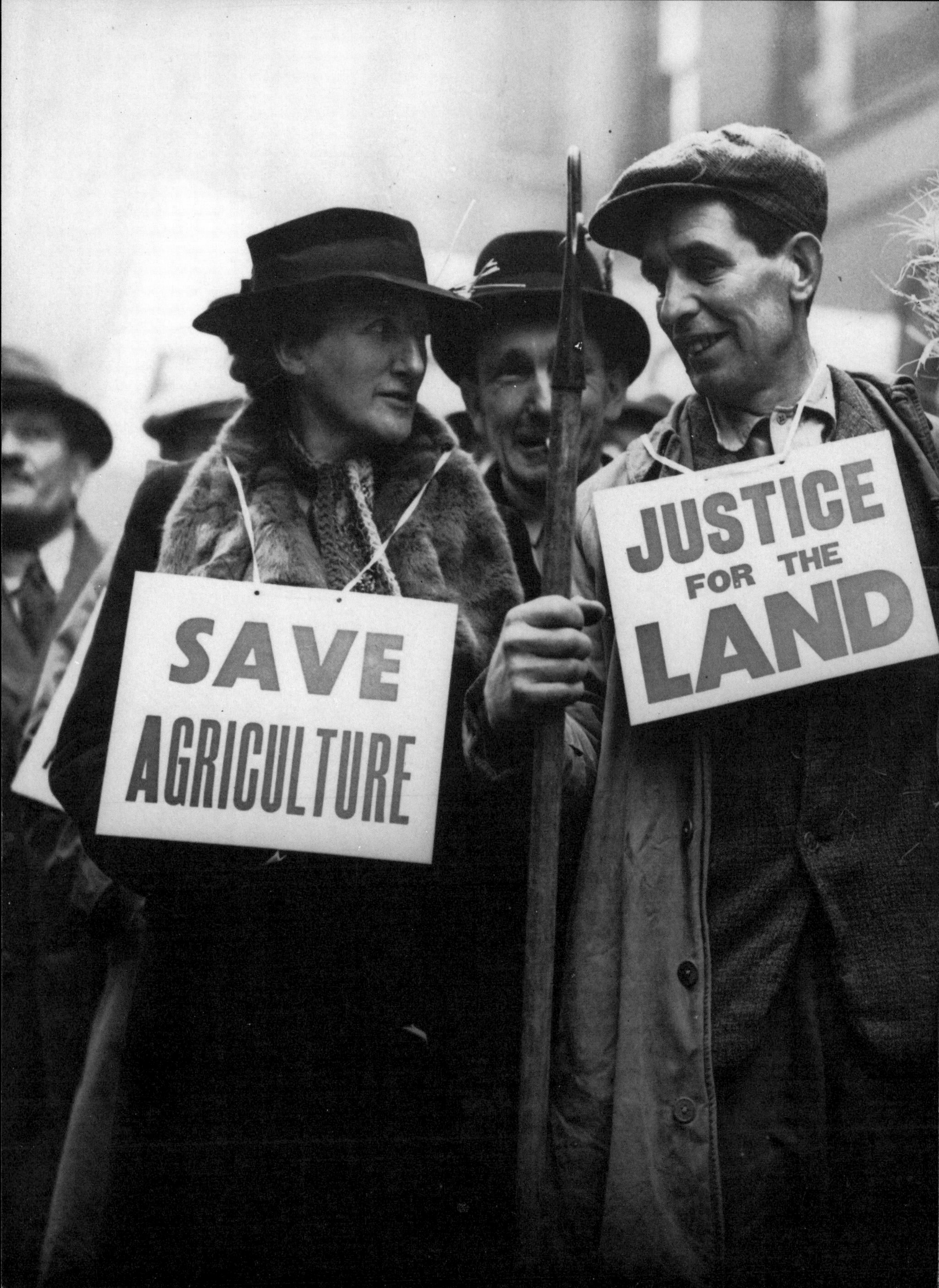
SAVE
AGRICULTURE
JUSTICE
FOR THE
LAND

87–88. Farmers and farm workers on a protest march to Westminster, February, 1939. At bottom right, Herefordshire hop pickers. The farmers asked for more Government support, their workers for better pay. "It is a scandal that the unemployed should be sleeping on the streets of London while we are crying out for workers", one of their representatives said.

Neglected Areas

89–92. The increased prosperity of the late Thirties was highly selective, in relation to both areas and occupations. If you were a Midlands car worker, things were not bad. If you worked in a Welsh mine, or a Scottish or North Eastern shipyard, they were very bad indeed. Government policy was to give as little help as possible. If industry in an area was depressed, that was bad luck.

The pictures show a derelict shipyard at Jarrow and the never-used ironworks at Blaenavon in Wales (left and below). On the right Cardiff workers pick over a rubbish dump, and the unemployed work their allotment. Such conditions, such lives, made angry men.

The Jarrow March

93. Jarrow, an undistinguished industrial town in the North East, became the symbol of the deepest misery, the most hopeless anger, of the period. Ellen Wilkinson, the little red-headed Labour firebrand of the period, called Jarrow the town that died. Over 80% of its people were unemployed, and when a deputation saw Walter Runciman, President of the Board of Trade, they were told that they would get no Government support. "Jarrow must work out its own salvation", Runciman said in a memorable phrase.

In 1936, Jarrow tried. The Jarrow March, or Crusade as some called it, took over a month to reach London, gathering support as it went.

94–95. Cooking up was sometimes done in the open. Sometimes there was a welcome from a Town Council, in other places bread and margarine in the local workhouse. Sympathetic doctors and medical students looked after the men. The outcome was a big Hyde Park meeting, banners, speeches, songs, a petition. And after that? Why, back to Jarrow.

The Way They Went on Living

96–98. There were fewer unemployed, but the number never went much below 2 million in the winter. Their plight remained the same, or even worsened. A few had glimpses of hope, like the Durham miner out of work for 14 years (top right) accepted as tenant for a cottage homestead near Reading. But these were the lucky ones. For most it was the dole queue, the Means Test, the daily look through the papers.

99–100. The slums remained. The building boom was real enough, but it affected only people above a certain income level, living in certain areas. Children played among rubble on Tyneside in 1938, as another generation had played ten years before. The picture below, from the film "Enough to Eat", made in 1936 by Arthur Elton for the Gas Light and Coke Company, suggests the companionable liveliness of some slum living.

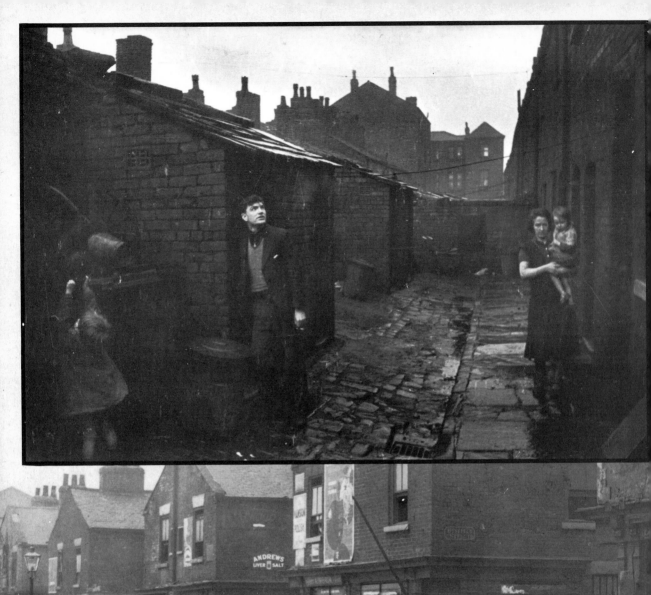

101–102. A back street in Wigan in the late Thirties, with the stones sloping down towards a central gutter, and the wretched desolation of a street in Leeds.

103. The rent here was only 14/6 a week for a living room, two small bedrooms and a kitchen. Not much. But the man was unemployed, and unemployment pay had hardly changed from the early Thirties. (See pages 20–1). The wife now got an extra shilling a week, and there was an extra shilling for each child. The total income here was 39/- a week to keep a family of six.

104. (*following pages.* A slum interior in Newcastle, 1938.)

Railway Problems

105-106. Long before nationalisation, the railway companies were complaining of Government restrictions. They had some reason. In their fight against competition from the rapid growth of road haulage, the railways struggled in bonds imposed by Parliament. They had "agreed rates", but these were mostly based on the value of the goods carried, while road hauliers based their prices on the cost of carrying the goods. The most valuable (and profitable) goods went by road, the cheapest (and least profitable) by rail. It is true also that the companies—with the notable exception of the Southern—did little to help themselves by electrification of lines and improvement of passenger services. The "Square Deal" campaign asked for changes in the law to allow the companies greater flexibility in making charges, particularly for freight.

CLEAR THE LINE !

ALL RIGHT IN GRANDFATHER'S DAY
Ancient regulations block the line to progress on the railways.

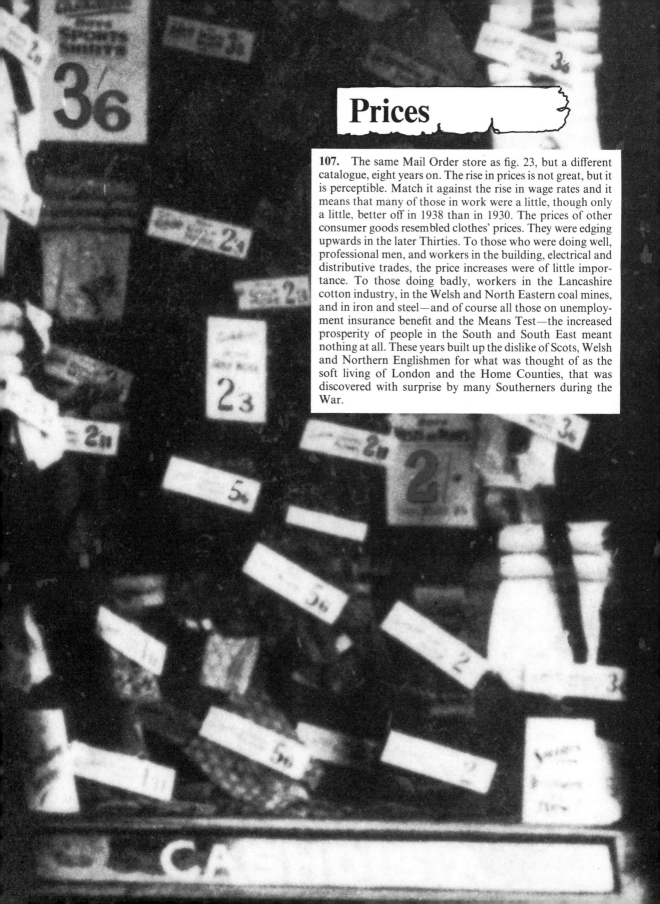

Prices

107. The same Mail Order store as fig. 23, but a different catalogue, eight years on. The rise in prices is not great, but it is perceptible. Match it against the rise in wage rates and it means that many of those in work were a little, though only a little, better off in 1938 than in 1930. The prices of other consumer goods resembled clothes' prices. They were edging upwards in the later Thirties. To those who were doing well, professional men, and workers in the building, electrical and distributive trades, the price increases were of little importance. To those doing badly, workers in the Lancashire cotton industry, in the Welsh and North Eastern coal mines, and in iron and steel—and of course all those on unemployment insurance benefit and the Means Test—the increased prosperity of people in the South and South East meant nothing at all. These years built up the dislike of Scots, Welsh and Northern Englishmen for what was thought of as the soft living of London and the Home Counties, that was discovered with surprise by many Southerners during the War.

Happy Styles—Happy Days—Happy Prices!

Just like Fine Linen

Model O 2440 (below)—The perfect Model for sunny days—and for Afternoon Wear, too, carried out in a fine quality heavy draping Imitation Linen with lovely slub effect, so good looking and perfect in wash and wear. In the ever-popular tailored style, with long rever collars to the smart double-breasted waistcoat effect bodice, showing a neat little pocket, and four unusually pretty buttons. Short sleeves, and a graceful skirt, with finely stitched seams from the "waistcoat" points, opening to the useful inverted pleats below the knee. Shades: Lupinblue, Lemon, Nil-green, Natural, Marina-green, White, Peach.

Women's Sizes....
Larger Sizes, 16/6
12/6

A "Highlight" for Holidays

Model O 2484—The loveliest Two-Piece—perfect for Holidays and smart enough for Town Wear, too! Made in a heavy quality Vogue Matt fabric, like silky linen, the Dress on "tailored" lines with neat square neck and well-cut skirt with pleat back and front. Button-trimmed tabs and an all-round belt match the elegant Coatee with its jaunty little stand collar, neat short sleeves, and "fall-away" fronts trimmed so charmingly with the newest Ciré braid in colour to match the Dress. Shades:
Saxe Dress with White Coatee.
White Dress with Saxe Coatee.
Navy Dress with White Coatee.
White Dress with Navy Coatee...
Can only be supplied as advertised.
20/-

ALL MODELS ON THIS PAGE TO FIT :
32 to 36 ins. Bust.
Up to 38 ins. Hips.
Lengths from neck to hem: 46 and 48 ins.

VERY SMART!

Ideal for Summer Comfort

Model O 2454—Figured Imitation Linen—there's no nicer material for sunny days! And you surely couldn't wish for a lovelier style—it has all the details of a genuine Model, and the perfect line that flatters every type of figure. Well-fitting collar with wide revers, short sleeves with tucked shoulders for military squareness, two pleated breast pockets, and buttons matching the buckle to the all-round belt. The skirt has a slim-fit line, with its graduated centre panel opening to the newest inverted pleat below. Ground shades of Harvest-gold, Powder-blue, and Mid Green......
10/11
Larger Sizes, 14/11

O 2440

O 2454

Model O 2485

FOR BEACH OR PROMENADE

(Model O 2485 above right)

Here's a Beach Frock with a double appeal—it's smart and it's sensible! Made to button right down the front, like a Coat—ideal for wear over your bathing costume or beach shorts—yet smart enough in material, style and finish for Promenade wear, and for sunny days at home. The heavy quality Ottoman Piqué is very prettily figured, and the wide revers, "squared" shoulders, and sleeve cuffs are piped in contrast, matching the smart buttons. There's a plain narrow belt also in the contrasting colour. Your holiday kit will not be complete without this useful Frock. Predominating shades: White/Red/Navy, White/Green/Orange, White/Green/Red......
15/-
Larger Sizes, 19/11

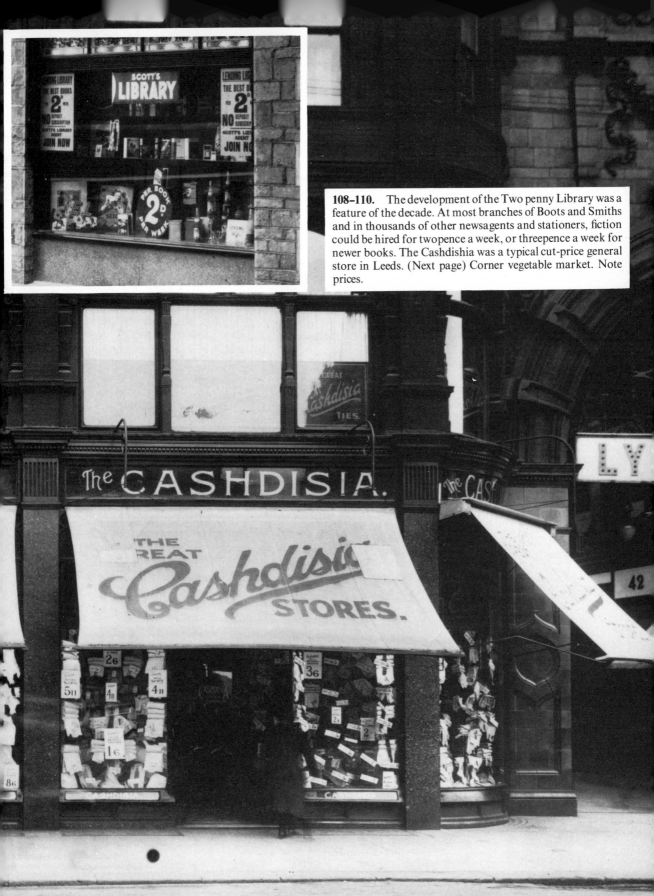

108–110. The development of the Two penny Library was a feature of the decade. At most branches of Boots and Smiths and in thousands of other newsagents and stationers, fiction could be hired for twopence a week, or threepence a week for newer books. The Cashdishia was a typical cut-price general store in Leeds. (Next page) Corner vegetable market. Note prices.

WATNEY COMBE REID & CO. LTD

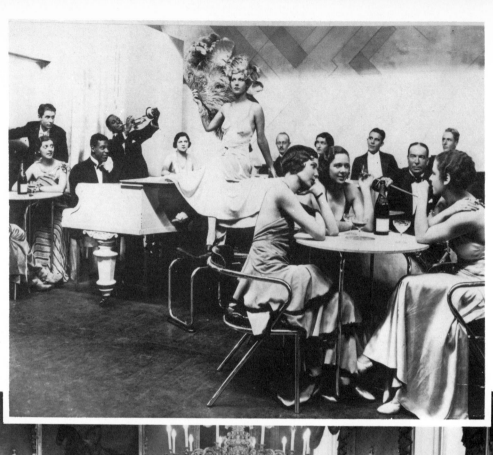

111–115. Noel Coward's *Cavalcade* was the escapist work par excellence of the decade. Another sort of escapism was represented by the League of Nations meeting here in St James's Palace. With each Hitlerian triumph the League's activities became more remote from reality. New roads were being driven through the countryside and cars moved along them at speeds which caused indignant protest. The 30 m.p.h. speed limit was introduced in 1935. Burnley's safety tram was a novelty of the period.

WAR APPROACHING

116. June, 1939. Fairey bombers under construction in the Austin works at Birmingham. With the acceptance of war as inevitable, and rearmament starting in earnest, the numbers of unemployed dropped dramatically.

117–118. August, 1938. Viscount Runciman (that same Runciman who had been so brutally dismissive of Jarrow's sufferings—see pages 90–91) leaves for Prague to "mediate" between the Czechoslovaks and the Sudeten Germans backed by Hitler. This mediation between the hens and the fox failed. Runciman's powers of persuasion proved no greater than his ability to do anything about Jarrow.

January, 1939. A typical consequence of the failure. Hore-Belisha, now War Minister, and faintly visible on the left, sees AA guns being made at the Royal Ordnance factory.

· ALL THIS WEEK ·
CHAMBERLAIN
THE
PEACEMAKER
SCREEN STORY OF BRAVE
GREATEST LIVING CITIZEN WHO ?"
HIS COURAGE STEADFASTNESS
AVERTED A WORLD CATASTROPHE

THE NEWS THEATRE

119–121. September, 1938. The Mad Hatter controls the tea party. Chamberlain, British Prime Minister, flies out to Munich, and returns believing that he has obtained "Peace With Honour". In fact he has simply sold out the Czechs, but this is not generally realised at the time. In and outside Parliament he is praised. A Birmingham cinema shows the "screen story of Birmingham's greatest living citizen". The policy is called appeasement by its opponents. A demonstration by the Communist-inspired Unemployed Workers Movement settles in uncompleted A.R.P. trenches and asks for work. Sir John Anderson was the Home Secretary, and "Bring Anderson to Eel" is a joke. The demonstrators said that they had caught eels in the watery trenches.

APPEASE THE UNEMPLOY
BRING ANDERSON -TO 'EEL!
BRING - ANDERSON - TO !
GIVE US WORK
GIVE US WORK ON A.R.P.!
GIVE US WORK ON A.R.P.!

122. The end of another Unemployed Workers Movement demonstration. The "coffin" of an unemployed man with the slogan: "Unemployed. No 'Appeasement'" is being taken away by the police.

123–125. July, 1939. Four hundred young Jews lucky enough to be allowed out of Germany and Austria, arrive in London. These are three children from the refugee train. A.R.P. trenches are dug in St James's Park, within sight of the German Embassy.

August, 1939. Children, ticketed and carrying gas masks, leave London. War is only days away.

126. Gas mask drill at school. These children make it look easy, but in fact the putting on and removal of gas masks proved too much for many small children.

127–128. September, 1939. War has been declared. Winston Churchill, the new First Lord of the Admiralty (detective bodyguard following) looks suitably solemn as he crosses the Horse Guards. A family, carrying gas masks, enters an air raid shelter. The shelters were much less uncomfortable than they looked from the outside.

129. September, 1939. Chamberlain, with his Parliamentary Private Secretary Sir Alec Douglas-Home, leaves Downing Street after announcing that England is at war with Germany. Douglas-Home carries a gas mask under his arm, and another—for his master?—in his hand.